Soul Dancer

Courtney Force

Courtney Force
Forcefield Healing LLC
Malibu, California
www.forcefield.energy

First edition self-published by Courtney Force. Cover design by Courtney Force. Editing by Courtney Force.

FOR YOU

this is for the dreamers
the feelers
the adventurers
the ones who want to change the world

it's for the outcasts
the ones who feel they don't belong
that think they're too much
or not enough
or sometimes both
at the same time

this is for the lovers
the ones with their hearts on their sleeve
the mothers sisters and daughters
the fathers brothers and sons
and it's for the ones who feel alone

this is for the sacredness inside of you
this is for your soul
this is for your remembering

this is for you

INTRODUCTION

Where do you go when you're lonely, lost, or hurting? Where do you go when you need inspiration, hope, or joy?

My answer has always been books. They have the power to transport you to another world, stir up emotions inside you and connect you to yourself, as well as all of humanity. Books have always been the key to the great wisdom that I seek.

My father is a poet. For as long as I can remember, he has expressed himself, his emotions, and his experiences in rhythm and rhyme. On birthdays I would often look forward to receiving his insightful poetry as much as I would any gift (though I did enjoy the cherry red mustang on my 16th birthday as much as any poem).

In college, I studied communication. I was no stranger to the power of words. Still, through the catalyst of San Diego State University, I learned how communication could open and close doors, cause both misunderstandings and healings, and change our entire world. Words can be used in many ways (to manipulate and distort reality, sure), but more importantly, words can be used to portray the complexities inside us, rewire our brains, and connect us to our deeper truths, as well as each other.

Words are spells, which is why we call the construction of words spelling. The ancient axiom, Abracadabra, while being fun to say, literally means, "I create as I speak."

In 2013, at the end of college, as I got ready to spread my wings and take flight into the real world, I experienced an intense, world-shattering spiritual awakening. Deeper esoteric truths, past life memories, clairvoyant and clairaudient abilities, empathy and intuition, and so much more opened up for me. I went through an intense dark night of the soul and reconnected to my truths, understanding reality in a whole new way.

During this time, I remembered that writing poetry is a big part of my purpose. I quit my social life (to a large extent) and focused on self-development. The poems from this time are the first ones you'll read in this book, including "Soul Dancer."

It has been a full-on journey since then. I've studied tarot, astrology, energy healing, past life regression therapy, soul memory discovery, breathwork, and yoga. I currently teach others how to connect with their soul in these profound ways through my business, Forcefield.

I would attribute my delay in publishing this book entirely to divine timing, which I trust above all else. Truthfully, however, there is a level of perfectionism that contributes to this book being nine years in the making, which is ok. I no longer work for my perfectionism. Now my perfectionism works for me.

I wrote these poems through that challenging period between 20 to 29 years old when we go on an often self-led journey to discover who we are and find our place in the world.

So, my dear reader, here we are.

My wish is that you find a piece of yourself in this book, a memory long forgotten, or a reclamation of who you are.

I imagine we'll get to know each other quite intimately through this book. You can't write poetry without sharing a piece of your heart and soul. There are times when that terrified me above all else, but now there is nothing I desire more.

Here is the alchemy I learned - to change the base emotions of fear, shame, depression, and more into the elevated ones of hope, love, and joy. Anyone can do this with enough time and energy devoted to understanding the process. The result is the manifestation of the life of your dreams, both on the outside and the inside.

Soul Dancer is a hero's journey (or rather, a heroine, if you will) into herself, the underworld, the heavens, her past, her future, and her present.

I hope these poems help you feel less alone. I hope they help you remember that we all feel similar emotions; we all hope and dream. We all laugh and cry. We are far more similar than we are different, and yet our differences deserve to be celebrated too.

Thank you for being here at this crazy time on planet Earth. Thank you for showing up even when your heart breaks, even when the weight of the world threatens to crush you. Even when _____. What is it for you? What is the unique way that you struggle with your reality? Thank you for doing that. Thank you also for thriving, smiling, and just being you. You matter.

Thank you to my family and my beloved soul mate for all the love and support they have poured into me over the years. I would not be who I am without you.

Thank you to my friends, teachers, and guides, both in the physical and the spiritual world.

Thank you to all the past versions of me that persevered to get me here.

Most of all, thank you to the Creator. I create because you created me. I have known you by many names throughout my life, but my love for you has never changed.

Thank you, Great Spirit. Thank you again.

With great love,

Courtney Force

TABLE OF CONTENTS

III. Self Discovery Has Many Stages

VI. In The End There Was Love

I. there has always been love

FULL MOON INSOMNIA

insomnia strikes
why tonight
two words
full moon

SOUL DANCER

come here soul dancer
let's whisper
about the cycles of the moon
pyramids built so long ago
and cities that lay in ruin

come here soul dancer
please tell me
stories small and large
of heroes villains heroines
and the gods of distant stars

come here soul dancer
find refuge
in the curves of my arms
i'll tell you of hope love loneliness
and how i feel you strongest of all

come here soul dancer
please hurry
these light years
have kept us apart

come here soul dancer
don't worry
i've saved you
this spot in my heart

THE MUSIC OF YOU

play me something
soft and slow
play me something
sweet
your breath
creates the timing
your heart
it keeps the beat
your eyes
they trace
subtle lines
on my skin
like worn out
guitar strings
your lips
on their own
create a melody
you don't even
open your mouth
to sing
the blink of your eyelids
maracas
your chest
rises and falls
with ease
your rhythm
your passion
your silence
the orchestra
that awakens me

IN BETWEEN WORLDS

the sun is slowly rising
and i'm still half asleep
dreaming of people and places
that share my memories

i sink into my solitude
and greet silhouettes of someones
who left imprints on my mind
freeze dried in time

reaching for the horizon
memories floating in the sky
visions slipping through my grasp
as reality materializes

if i could chase these footprints back
through strides of space and time
i feel i'd find you smiling there
exactly as you're smiling in my mind

TWISTED SHEETS

we'd toss and turn
in twisted sheets
with dreams of what
we thought we'd be

we've missed our turn
a thousand times
a memory reel
each other's eyes

ALMOST LOVER

i wanted to lasso
your spirit
anchor your heart
to mine
tie our souls
together
interlock our hands
till the end of time

i wanted
ever so dearly
to give our love
a chance

but you'll have to understand
my darling
i had to leave
when our demons
started to dance

OCEAN CARESS

i once heard
a sea-locked rock
say to a wave

even after
all our suns
and moons
together
you still find ways
to touch me
that I've never
felt before

A STUDY OF CHANGE

the first time i met change was in purgatory
he was with the devil himself
crunching numbers and comparing tables
trying his best to explain
why things couldn't ever just stay the same

the second time i met change
he was with the greatest philosophers of every age
telling them that
even ideas change with time
galileo copernicus and pythagoras smirk
as they look down on a round earth orbiting a sun
aristotle stands at the center of the galaxy and says
fine but at least logic remains
to which heraclitus replies
no the only true constant in life is change

my final encounter with change he was on trial
a class action lawsuit
they had him for malicious intent
love happiness abundance peace glory among others
wanted to know why
their best manifestations
their favorite moments and memories
couldn't ever last

charles darwin is change's first defendant
he takes the podium and simply states
you ungrateful bastards
change made you what you are

TRADE OFF

somewhere
between
the person
i was
and the person
i became
i lost you
and found me

ESCAPE

i wonder
if you ever feel
trapped
by walls and ceilings
suffocated
beneath clothes
make up
and worldly expectations

i wonder
if you ever feel
claustrophobic
between big buildings
and big egos
longing to be
naked
weightless
and free
in a world that has forgotten
what those words really mean

i wonder
if you ever dream about
running away
and if you do

i wonder
if you ever dream about
taking me
with you

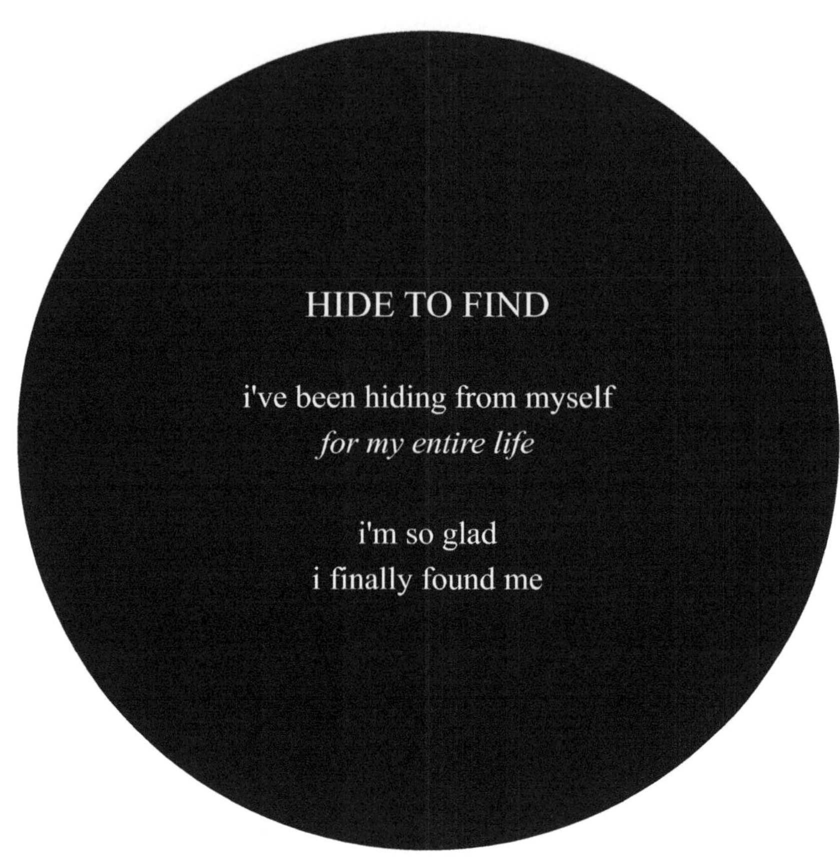
HIDE TO FIND
i've been hiding from myself
for my entire life
i'm so glad
i finally found me

FRAGILE

we were fragile little things
with such soft skin
tender lips
delicate bones
slow beating hearts

vulnerable eyes
invite you in

blood is thin
and oxygen light
the cruelest demons
kill you from the inside

CONSTRAINTS

walls
rules
and
restrictions
don't work well on
vixens

boundaries become cages
fences made for containment
barbed wire separation
and chain link annexation

my mind wanders free
in
wide
open
spaces

A WISH A DREAM

i know
not a single thing
more beautiful
than this

that the darkness
inside me
would marry
the light
dance together
in perfect harmony
and never again
mention the word
opposite

CRASH LANDING

i found you
in crop circles
and meteorites

stardust in your hair
and asteroids
under your fingernails

you'd just taken
the last comet
from anywhere

you kept repeating
i don't belong here
i don't belong here

i told you
none of us do

we're all just
visitors
aliens
strangers

we're all just
passing through

PREDATORS

lovers
drop their hearts
at my feet

so when
you found me
with blood dripping
from my lips
you told me
that it wasn't my fault
that people like us
should come
with warning labels

i smiled at you
sheepishly
my eyes begging the question
what are we actually supposed to do
with our huge capacities
for love

i just hope
it all amounts to more
than a few hundred
devoured hearts

II. in the beginning there was hope

COVERED EARTH

i hate walking on concrete
while the earth
suffocates
beneath my feet
longing
to feel them
on her

FIND THE ART

in everything
there is art
a poem
a song

the masterpiece
sleeps silently
below the surface
waiting for someone
to see it

brush off the dust
give it a face
a voice
bring it to life

ROMANTIC ANTICS

the flame
of my candle
dances
to kunzel

the never-ending waltz

and i laugh
at my romantic heart
for she would jump
into that glass jar
and dance with him too

WAIT FOR FATE

why have me wait
when i know what i am meant for
and what is meant for me

why have me wait

yes i address you fate
again why have me wait

and fate
she doesn't answer
she makes me wait

and i wait
and i wait
and i say
fate
why make me wait

she doesn't answer
and in her silence
i shutter

you make yourself wait

FLOWERS FOR A FRIEND

you ask where have you been
well i am with you now
no what about the times before
you weren't around
you let us down

surely you speak with sincerity
in truth where have i been
if i owe one thing to this world
it's explanations to my friends

my heart she is a garden
and my fragile plants
withering away
i put her through
such harsh conditions
indeed i am to blame

and so i needed time
to sow some seeds
and plant some crops
love and care for myself
must always be at the top

and look my dearest friend
my efforts have not been in vain
i spent that time on my own garden
to stand here with you today

these flowers are
my love my sadness
my joy my hope my fear
i grew them with the sun of my soul
i watered them with my tears

but alas my garden has never been for me
for while i know i must nurture myself
i also did it for others to see

and yes my friend
these flowers i hold
i grew them all for you
yes my friend
i know i know
i really missed you too

CLOCKWORK

time

i do not know
if you go
fast or slow
or maybe both
at the same

time

SANDCASTLES

we built sandcastles
out of the fragments of our dreams
and wept for the seashells they once were

we created oceans with each salty tear
and we built towers out of our promises
resurrected mountains with our joy

love and laughter
filled our world with life
and we felt invincible
you and i

but soon wind and wave
came to take our castle back to sea
and then you and me
we understood
how delicate castles can be

as all our love came crashing down
into piles of rubble and sand
we marveled at how quickly
worlds collapse

how fragile
the creations of man

KASAI

passion burns like fire
i say
you would have it
be put out

nay
you say
just contained

ah
we speak
of different fires

THE HUMAN RACE

why call we the human race
who do we race

i will tell you

we race time

need i say
that the odds
are not in our favor

our condition
the human condition
is to be so preoccupied
with chasing the next present moment
that we neglect to remember

we are living the only one

OUR HEART STRINGS

you never understood
t h e   m i l l i o n s   o f   i n v i s i b l e   s t r i n g s
that connected your heart to mine
and mine to yours

and you never understood
how energy works
in that when your heart smiled
t h e   e c s t a t i c   v i b r a t i o n s
that translated through our heart strings
caused my heart to smile too

similarly our hearts have
cried in unison
loved in unison
doubted in unison
hoped in unison

even still when i feel
a   p a n g   o f   m i s s i n g   y o u
in my heart
i do not doubt that
you just felt it too

MOONLIGHT ILLUMINATED TEARS

some scars heal
but they never stop hurting
there's a piece of you
in me
that just won't fade away

some memories slip through fingers
into the open hands of time

some memories stick forever
i cannot shake you from my mind

sitting on a colony of grass
knees drawn halfway to your chest
lips trembling from loss and fear

i have tried so hard
but can't forget
your moonlight illuminated tears

MY ANCESTOR'S LEGACY

there's some
swell of belonging
upon realizing
just how much
love was made
for me to be
standing here

millions of people
like a tangled web
knotted tree
passing the secrets
of life and love
down to me

TRUST IN LOVE
how much
you love someone
is limited
by how much
you can trust them
with your heart

WILDFIRE SOULS

when you love to play with fire
you're destined to get burned
for a girl with fire in her soul
the flame no longer hurts

paper hearts burn too fast
and they're never quite as fierce

stone hearts are awfully boring
and they don't really know how to feel

so i dreamt of a
fireproof lover
fire eater
fire drinker
to swallow my blazing spirit
and furnace my wildfire soul

oh but you
i've loved boys like you
with icebox hearts
so i know how to arouse a spark
somewhere in the dark
of a stiff frozen heart

my soul melts your tundra
your equilibrium can't take the heat
if i spontaneously combust
you're exploding in flames with me

LIVE BOLDLY

some hid their imperfections
under layers upon layers
of masks and disguises

she wore her issues
boldly
on the outside
like jewelry

pearls of sadness
rubies of anger
gold chains of insecurity
adorned her eclectic soul

she'd say
the only thing to be ashamed of
is shame itself
this is who i am
this is who i want to be

LONG WAY GONE

our paths
diverged
miles ago
and now there's
mountains
between us

THE SUNRISE IN YOUR EYES

let's finger paint
with the clouds

i'll dip them in
the colors of your eyes
and light them
with your smile

the gods will envy
our sunrise

OPPOSITES ATTRACT

you were simple
and i was not

you liked what you liked
and didn't like what you didn't like
and right was right
and wrong was wrong
and black was black
and white was white
and that was that
and this was this
and what about gray
no gray doesn't exist

except in my world
where gray does exist
and there's black
but also magenta and orange
and sometimes fuchsia
and there's white
but also blue and lavender
and sometimes periwinkle
and right is right
except for when there's bad intentions
or a bad outcome
or people getting hurt
and wrong is wrong
except for when there's good intentions
or a good outcome
or people healing from it

and sometimes i like what i like
but sometimes i don't like it
and sometimes i don't like what i don't like
but sometimes i do like it
and that is not always that
and this is not always this
sometimes that is this
and this is that

so what were two people
like you and i to do

try and fail
try and fail
try and fail

TIME TO CLIMB

you got so busy
building your safety net
that you forgot to build your tower

that hammock may be comfortable
but don't forget
world changer
destiny still has planned
great heights for you to climb

POTENTIAL MAN

i never loved you
i loved my over romanticized version
of the man you could be

SOMETHING REAL

i built you pedestals
out of my childhood ideals
of prince charming
soul mates
and star crossed lovers

but ideas in time
grow their own wings
and i was never meant to be
a songbird in a cage
stuck with prince charming

and you know
i'm a rebel of fate
so what would i gain
from a destiny intertwined
meant to be soul mate

stars may cross like paths do
but the sun is my only star
and you are my only you

when our pedestals took flight
i thought you'd surely fall
but you grew your own wings
and you rose above them all

CONVERSATIONS WITH THE GURU

guru
i am
looking
for something
what will happen
when i find it

a moment
for contemplation

you will begin looking
for something else

III. self-discovery has many stages

BRINGING SHADOWS TO LIGHT

there are times
when the spark
goes out
and my soul shudders
at the dark and the cold

when my eyes finally adjust
i notice at once
my shadow self
wears this gruesome grin
like she's playing a game
that i don't know
and that she intends to win

there in the black
i can't seem to call back
the things that i knew in the light
but the thing about morning
it comes without warning

now my shadow self dances in light

UNIVERSAL ONENESS

cosmic connection
    where every other being
        is a perfect reflection
            of your own soul

your own heart beating
    the moment of meeting
        is a divine reconvening
            of all that is

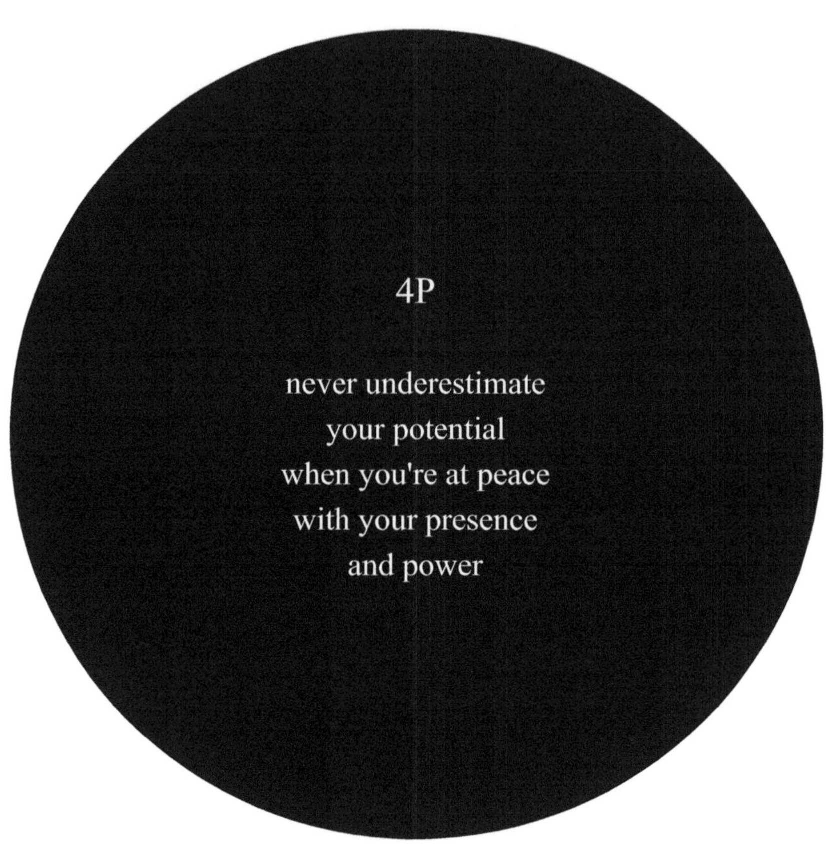
4P
never underestimate
your potential
when you're at peace
with your presence
and power

PASSION FOR LIFE

i never died of passion
no

passion pushed me
and pulled me
and inflicted one too many wounds
but passion was never capable
of taking my life

the true killer was mediocrity
yes

the boring and mundane
fired bullets at my soul
with simple phrases like
everyone else is doing it
it's ok to settle
this is normal
you'll be fine

and when i was lying there
on my death bed
my soul in purgatory
it was passion that resuscitated me

and to passion
i owe my life

SURRENDER AND CONTROL

you can't force
the words to flow
you can't make
a relationship grow
you won't succeed
before your time
you can't compel
your light to shine

surrender to
the process
the flow
the path

surrender to
the grace inside
the hope and faith
that lasts

know that there's a plan for you
you're co-creating it
with each choice
know that your destiny is divine
listen to your inner voice

rise to every occasion
don't shrink
when life gets hard
the discomfort
and the loneliness
are just another part

of the courage it takes
to see your dreams
come to life
before your eyes

be discerning
and aligned
in the choices
you make
stay true
to the knowing
inside

continue
to open your heart
even when
it hurts
continue
to trust your vision
even when
you feel unsure

the light of your soul
will guide you home
the joy of your life
will overflow
and as you live
in ease and grace
within the world
you'll find your place

ME AS ME

searching
seeking
scanning
solitude
someone show me
something synonymous
something similar
same as me
sister soul
somewhere

SECRET SELF
the things
you don't know
about someone
say more
about them
than all the things
you do know
combined

WHICH PART

i have no desire
to be your entire world
but let me be your island
your tropical paradise getaway
sunshine skin salt margarita

i have no desire
to be your entire world
but let me be your asteroid
your big dream shooting star
flaming meteor galaxy traveler

i have no desire
to be your entire world
but let me be your desert oasis
your fresh sparkling
life giver life saver life maker

i have no desire
to be your entire world
but let me be
your favorite part

ECLIPSE ME

divinely inspired
you planted celestial kisses
on my flesh and bone body
transcendental daydreams
after smoking stardust
bathing in meteor showers
and soul dancing
for the rest of the night
we were manifestations
of the galaxies
in homo sapien form
and when we finished
i swear i heard zeus say that
in moments like these
he longs to be human

FOR A MOMENT I WAS LOST

the words find me
broken
hiding in a corner

how did you lose your voice
strong speaker
word weaver
destined leader
you
who asked to hear
the god's speech
so you could share it
how did you forget how to speak

the fears start in on me
so i don't blame them
the obvious suspect

of course
it is fear that
holds our tongue
paralyzes our minds
keeps us captive
to our own insecurities
and of course
we must all fight our own demons
while in persevering
as in healing
light fights on our side
and the journey liberates the soul

PURE RELIGION

throw me in the water
i've always loved to swim
when i get dragged down and tumbled around
i'll find the strength i hold within

baptize me in the water
in the name of what's sacred and true
show me the way back home
i long to be reunited with you

dry me off with sunlight
show me the way to my path
we'll burn all the evil that steps in the way
and when it's reborn
we'll embrace them and laugh

take all the fear from my heart
put all my trust in the one
unite me with brothers and sisters in love
we're changing the world
and won't stop till we're done

keep my feet planted firmly on the earth
my roots reach deep in the ground
i belong with the flowers
i dance with the wind
and the walls in my heart
just keep tumbling down

BEFORE SUMMER ENDS

you were the smell of a barbecue
on the light easy breeze
of a warm summer night
while i sat in your passenger seat

i was the fresh squeezed lemonade
that you drank with your eyes closed
while the easy conversation of our friends
played muffled in the background

we were surprisingly domestic
for how wild our spirits are

being with you was always an adventure
an all-day bike ride to a secret spot
only we knew about

but we were more than metaphors
more than either of us bargained for
we were something so real
we had to catch our breath
and slow down to really believe it

and i really believed in you
i believed in us so much

until i didn't

summer is over
and nobody's barbecuing anymore

LOST IN THE CITY OF ANGELS

where are you now

i lost you in bright lights and traffic
i lost you in skyscrapers that concrete jungle
i lost you in the same place i found you
but you haven't been there since
i know because i've been looking

i guess i'll just say that i miss you

you the city at sunrise
as everyone else wakes up
bustling busy burdened

you the city at sunrise
as i roll over lazily
to rest my head on your chest

you the kiss on my forehead
you the strong arms around me
you the home that i made here
with you i felt safe

but i guess buildings do collapse without a strong foundation
and we always did have structural issues

so now as i stand here in the rubble of our love
i can't help but wonder
where are you now
i think i'd like to find you again

TAKE THE FIRST STEP

how magical
could your world be
if you left your tower
and went on
that grand adventure
you've been dreaming of

STAY FOUND

i'm stealing back my smile
abandoning guilt at the ocean's altar
and asking angels
if i may borrow their wings

all i really want is a glimpse of tomorrow
but if i can't have that
then all i really want is to feel complete now

step outside of space and time
abandon all thoughts and ideas
that confine me here
there's a better me out there
she says she sees my soul
and it is still golden light

if the sun looks different
every time he sets
then why do i expect myself
to always stay the same

abandon shame
embarrassment
judgment
rage
embrace the inner child
and tell her too
that whatever path she may choose
it will always be ok

HALF-HEARTED

faded smiles
from passerby
i want to shake them
all alive

when does one
become alright
with living
just a fraction
of a life

NUMB

all of creation hangs by a thread
my heart beats the tango
but i have
forgotten how to dance
forgotten how to sing
forgotten how to scream

at night i dream
of being naked
dancing around campfires
howling at the moon

but i wake up
to my same routine
wash my face
brush my teeth
go to my office
come home

and wonder
why i don't recognize
the person that i see

how do you remember
how to dance

when there's
no more campfires
no more tribes
no more safe spaces to sing

A BEAUTIFUL DISASTER

i'm slowly coming undone
unraveling strands
of sunset colored threads
and blowing dandelion memories
to the wind
please don't trip
over the abandoned fragments of me

i'm spiraling into control
i have chaos in a choke hold
but he has three hands around my neck

we smile at each other
because we share a fixation
with taking people's breath away

i'm my own favorite type of disaster
balancing on one foot
with my glass bones
and my paper mache heart
i'm an accident waiting to happen
please don't tip the scale

there's a 49% chance
i become something truly beautiful
and a 51% chance
i break every glass bone in my body
and set my heart on fire

but i'm still betting on me

THE CROW SPOKE

how could it be
how could it be
the day the crow
turned its head
looked at me
cackling
probing
questioning

why do you want roots
when you have wings

BEFORE THE SKY FALLS

there are 3 types of people in the rain:
those that bring an umbrella
those that cover their head cursing the sky
and those that like the way the rain feels on their face

i've always been the latter
so it should come as no surprise
that i smile in every type of weather

i wanted to tell you everything

like the way the chrysanthemums looked
on the back porch of the family home
i used to visit in my dreams

like the way the sunlight stained
the bleach white innocence of a young girl
studying flowers
and running through swamps all day

i wanted to tell you about the freedom
my soul imagined in its youth

but i forgot that words can get lost in poetry
not so different from the way
they've been battered down and broken
by anger and hatred
abused and misconstrued
by empty promises and lies
and squashed under the weight
of foul inhuman systems like racism and evil

but still
i wanted to tell you everything

like how i still visit the back porch
of that family home
in my dreams
and sometimes on somber summer nights
you meet me there

i wanted to tell you about how
light codes are like back roads
pathways to our soul

and that little girl
in her bleach white innocence
she could never be corrupted
for she was writing her own story:

the perseverance of the eternal soul

because every inner child
that survived
will tell you that
if it rains on your parade
you can find a way to dance in it

THE FIRST CHAPTER OF RECLAMATION

i grew up
outside of my own bones
on carpet and concrete
the earth begged to reclaim me

but she refused to make a deal with the devil

so the story goes like this
at 24 years old
i came home to my own body
realized this vessel is mine
i chose to be here
i agreed to this
refuse to play victim
i'm on my journey
i wrote this with intention

my heart knows the immigrant's story
she lays awake with my soul at night
and they moan the migration song
what have you done with my people

growing up on stolen land
educated on lies
where have you buried the truth
sold fake dreams
empty promises
and gilded advice
yet still i refuse to close my eyes

no i was not born outside of my bones
yes this society raised me there

here sign on the dotted line
courtney force
the corporation

abandon ship
this body
will have no other
ownership
than my own soul

PACKED UP AND MOVING ON

the sun's setting on palm trees
it's magic hour
and our little nest is eye level to the sea
that endless plane

the last rose blooms on our balcony tonight
tomorrow we'll be gone
off to another city a new home

today marks our last day
for tomorrow we must say
farewell to our first hideaway
our safe haven
this secret escape for our souls

this place that's seen our love grow
now in boxes
and sure i've always been sentimental
but this is more than just romantic ideals
of playing house husband and wife
this is more than just poetry
together we've built a life

and when these dreams are distant memories
and memories faint whispers on the breeze
when this chapter closes
and the next chapter opens
revealing our destinies
i will hold these moments sacred
the world shared between you and me

RECLAMATION PART 2

don't be afraid
to shine more light
to allow in more love
to dig deeper
into the depths
of your soul
to be more open
to life's possibilities

there are miracles waiting
on the other side of your fears

there is purpose hidden
underneath your pain

there is so much opportunity in life
just waiting for you to open to it

open to it

BE GUIDED

you've come so far
you're doing great
hold your head up high
accept your fate
the road is long and hard
it's true
the path not easy to walk
but look at you
you're showing up
and speaking truth
you're living in bliss
and allowing feelings to
rise and fall
and change and be
your heart is pure
your soul is free
your journey blessed
know this is true
you have a whole team
looking out for you
you're doing it
you're going far
we honor you
you shine like the stars
nobody else
is quite like you
there's something unique
in all you do

the truth of who
you're meant to be
is shining now
for all to see
keep embodying
your truth with grace
keep shining your light
and showing your face
laugh it all off
feel it all through
let it all be
we're so proud of you

KUNDALINI RISING

there’s a snake
at the base of my spine
sleeping

you dance around it
at night
don’t wake the dragon

when you hear the call
of the wild divine
follow it

it may

crack you open
light your life on fire
make you mad

but it's the only thing in life
truly worth doing

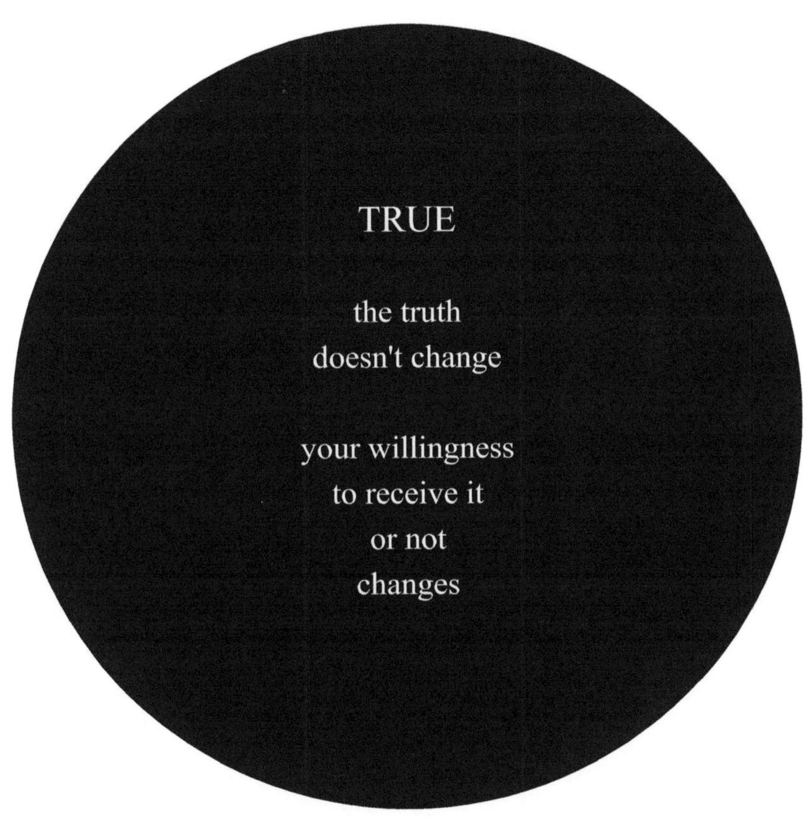
TRUE
the truth
doesn't change
your willingness
to receive it
or not
changes

ANCESTRAL HEALING

the pagan in me
married the christian
so never again will i be bitter
about the mistakes of somebody else's ancestors

i am a melting pot
the european crusader
falls at the feet of
my 4 times great grandmother
who died on the trail of tears
now you know the battle i have
with this ancestral fear

mistrust
there is no winner
in the game of war
both sides bleed
both sides sin
both sides pass on
a different type of pain
to their children

all my life i've struggled to look in the mirror
too dark for my light friends
too light for my dark friends
too confusing for strangers
that just had to stop me on the street
excuse me what's your ethnicity
no you don't have the right to bother me
i'm deep in the process of reclaiming my lost history

don't shame me
don't try to put me in a box
i will break free every time
exotic is a compliment
not when you desperately want to fit in

white privilege
comes in many forms
i get quiet enough to hear
my own shining through
sure i am lots of things
but yes i am white too

take off the masks
reclaim the truths
of sumiko kasai
my grandma from japan
who lied about being half white
the lost names of my great grandparents
lost stories

the erasure of civilizations
genghis khan
burning libraries of ancient wisdom
who gave you this right
who gave you this twisted desire
to destroy the light

well what i've come to know is
it's never black and white

HEALING THE PAST

i've been in the fire
more times than i can count
and i've danced with desire
until my legs gave out
and i've collapsed into ashes
laughing at the sky
and if there's one thing that i've learned
the truth will rise in time

PROPHECY

our hearts remember the way
and our souls long for the day
when we're united again as one
brothers and sisters under the sun

it's true nothing can keep us apart
the journey has already started
back to where we began
united again as one soul fam

even those who do not yet see
long for what we will be
so no one will be forgotten
we will all make it back to the garden

the day has been written
love will always win
so cast aside your fear
and hold each other near

don't allow hate
to ever separate
you from one another
your sisters and your brothers

our hearts will lead the way
the truth in the words we say
in the end love will overcome
and we will all be one

DIVINE DUALITY

i've worshiped at the altar
of the god and goddess
inside every person i have ever met
so you will never be able to convince me
that every single soul is not divine

i know too much about good and evil
to believe anything other than that
we all have both inside us
you aren't fooling me pretending
you're just love and light

i will look at your darkness
and love you there too

i built my demons a temple
and they became angels
no longer cast out of paradise
they remembered their birthright
they remembered deep inside them
they too are divine

i picked up the broken pieces of my heart
and made a mosaic
my body is my temple
these scars are my battle wounds
i am a survivor
and every painful experience i ever had
made me stronger

if i know one thing about me
it's this
i will persevere

every single time

i
fall
burn
collapse into ashes
disappear into oblivion
become nothing
become everything
rip up the old contracts
sign new ones

every single time

i will rise again

DREAMERS ARE GONNA DREAM

if we could live
on flowers and daydreams

if we could bottle up sunrises
and drink them like they were wine

if we could hold each other's souls
more than just flesh
if we could touch each other
where it really counts

then maybe the earth could return
to the garden of eden
we could end kal yuga early
all beings everywhere could know
that the balance of light and darkness
is the ultimate truth
and love will always win

if we could see each other
for the brothers and sisters
that we truly are

we could make the earth a better place
we could end the whole rat race
we could truly make a change
rise up out of all this pain
and live in harmony
for the rest of our days

PARTS OF YOU

you can spend
your whole life
denying your
true nature

but when something
is part of you
it will always
be part of you

ALCHEMICAL TRANSFORMATION

like the phoenix
we rise
almighty isis urges
do not cover your eyes
you're more powerful now
than you even realize
children of the earth
ocean sun wind and skies
you have a purpose here
don't fall into the lies
the false agenda and programming
created for your demise
remember you are divine
we all hear your cries
we all hear your hearts
we all know you're wise
awaken to the divinity
buried deep down inside
unburnt from the fire
transformed to new heights
what no longer serves you
must stay behind
in the fire it dies
you are much greater
you are the prize
your soul is pure gold
the alchemy that's inside
rise from the ashes now
rise phoenix rise

WOMAN'S SONG

come now daughter
sacred daughters
come on home now
to the seat of your soul

come now sister
sacred sisters
we have fields to roam
and stories to be told

come now mother
sacred mothers
you've birthed your life
and gave your dreams a home

come now elder
sacred elders
your ancient words of wisdom
are medicine for our souls

come now spirit
sacred spirits
your eternal light
will shine forever more

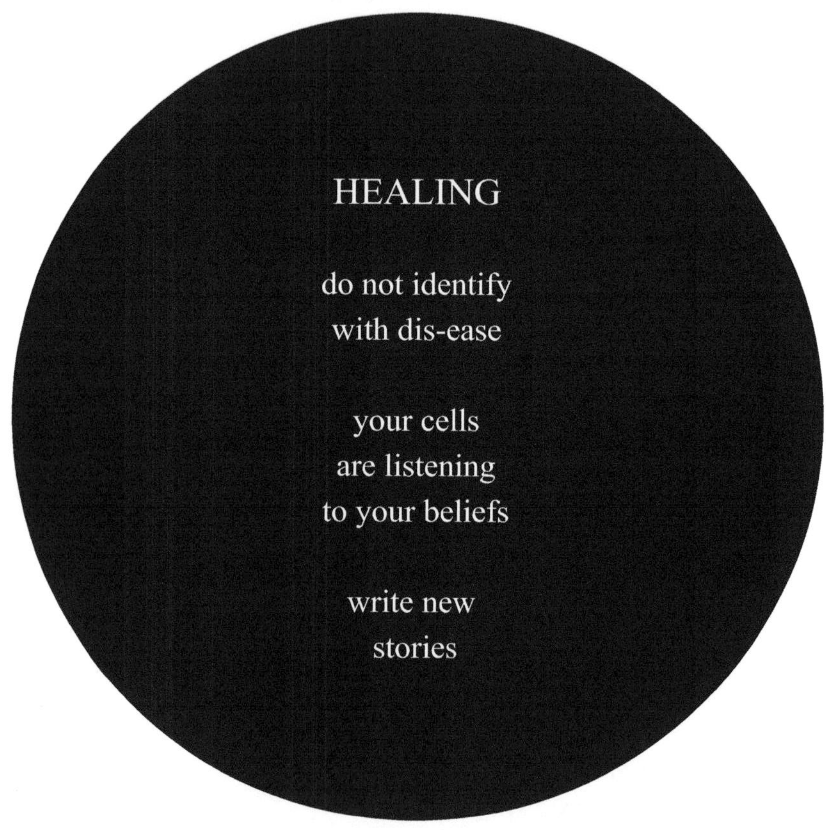

HEALING

do not identify
with dis-ease

your cells
are listening
to your beliefs

write new
stories

FORCE-FIELD

i'm growing
into my name

thank the growing pains

i stretched
and jumped
and pounded my fists
against the ground
to get here

me
who became a
contortionist
twisting
every which way
to fit into
society's expectations

dropped that act
i forgot that script
wrote a new story
reclamation

i'm growing
into my name
it expanded
to make room
for me

IV. in the middle there was faith

FLY CHILD FLY

trust the process
trust the path
believe there is
a grace that lasts

remain balanced
in all you do
remain aligned
with what's pure and true

strive to reach
the highest heights
and handle the depths
with courage and fight

you'll find friends
from all around
messengers from heaven
their love abounds

receive all of life
with an open heart
finish what your soul
calls you to start

be discerning
see what's real
be brave enough
to let yourself feel

have fun
enjoy your time
the treasures of life
you're sure to find

you're a child of god
made from the stars
you're a child of earth
you can handle what's hard

you were made
for these changing times
trust in your soul
don't rely on your mind

there's a balance to be found
within all things
get out of the cage now
trust in your wings

HER

the earth is a woman
sacred mother
maternal nature
matter
we are made of earth
we matter

SACRED REBELS

let's wage war on the streets

destroy the concrete
that tries to separate
the earth from our feet

take off our clothes
and remember how it feels
to be free

release expectations
of how we think
things should be

take in the wisdom
and medicine
from that ancient tree

re-learn simple truths
from the flowers
and the bees

find a new type
of faith and trust
in this sweet release

become living proof
that life will guide us
through our destinies

CHANGING TIDES PART 1

meet me at low tide
by the water's edge

speak to me about
ebbs
and flows
and smooth transitions

tell me
that it's ok
to go on
and when you want to
look back

fondly tending to memories
never forgetting
those precious rose colored day dreams
moments that were once
or moments that never will be

the tides
are constantly changing
and so are we

our dreams
rise up
on the mists of the sea

our visions
float on to a new day
a new future
something beyond our reach

the past
stretches behind us
the future
stretches before us
but right now
it's just you and me
right here
with a love
as boundless
and abundant
as the sea

i cherish this moment
i cherish these memories
graciously surrendered
to life's mysteries

i cherish my time
with you now

because by high tide
i'll be gone

SELF LOVE

someone i love
once told me
i had

eyes like a jaguar
eyes like a black hole
eyes like a thousand suns

someone i love
once told me
i could

light up the whole world
with my smile
and i believed them

so i learned to love myself
the way they loved me

i became
my own muse
my own lover
my own home

reclaimed my body
forgave myself
for all the ways i let her down

let my soul
lead the way

let my heart
feel however she wants to feel

let my mind
rest and be ready
just rest and be ready

and i discovered that
i am a jaguar
i am a black hole

i have the power of a thousand suns inside me
and i will shine my light wherever i go

i want to go everywhere

no more apologies
no more excuses
no more masks

just raw
and real me
ready for whatever
life has in store

DICHOTOMY

some days
i feel like
the whole entire ocean
and other days
i just feel lost at sea

A NEW REALITY

how many times
have you let fear

take control of
your soul
quiet you
silence you
put you in a box
that's not the right size for you

break free

HOW TO CATCH A BUTTERFLY

alright you guys
so you know
you can't really catch a butterfly right
if you do
she'll probably die
because she was made to fly
free across the sky
but if you want
the beauty of a butterfly
in your life
then here's what you can try

step 1
never catch her
cage her
or contain her

step 2
admire the way she flies
so free across the sky
not worried about wrong or right
a pure expression of what's inside
see the soul behind her eyes
as she dances for the light
let the love burn bright
feed her the sweet nectar of your life
play in her soul's shine
as you help her spirit thrive
never ask her why
and never try to tie her down

step 3
know when the love is ripe
know when the magic is right
give her your precious time
watch her reach new heights
floating along the light

step 4
admire her one last time
remember
she needs to fly
hold her
but not too tight
then
kiss her
good bye

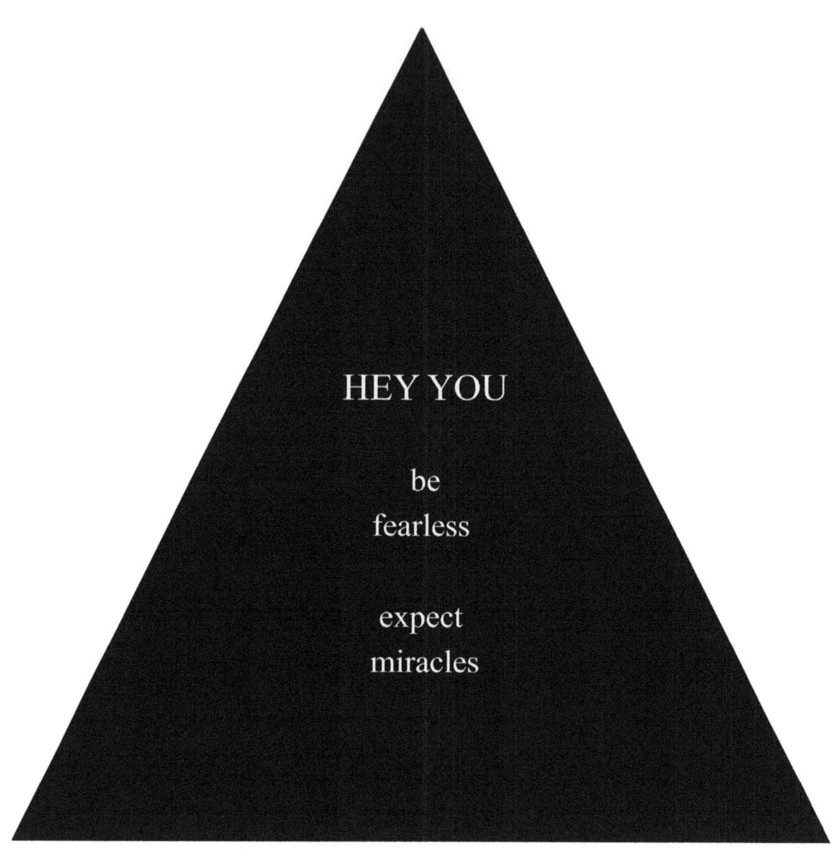
HEY YOU
be
fearless
expect
miracles

READ THIS WHEN YOU FEEL LET DOWN

beautiful heart

your feelings
are not your burden

your capacity for love
is not your curse

your ability
to connect
and trust
and see
the beauty
in every person
is not naivety

it is your strength

trust it
follow it
guard it
and allow it
to lead you home

home to your own soul

A HERO'S JOURNEY

in every thing
there is an ebb and flow
sometimes you shrink
sometimes you grow
the sun sets into darkness
then it rises and glows

we glorify the light
and crave its warmth
but forget that the darkness
doesn't require a torch
to sit with the pain
to watch the demons dance
to observe our lonely thoughts
to see our missed chances
to not run away and hide
or constantly seek the light
but allow the darkness to teach us
of the mysteries found deep inside

we're all fighting battles
we're all waging wars
seeking peace in our hearts
as we open secret doors
and face the monsters inside
with bravery in our hearts
because what's inside of us
are all vital parts
they each make us whole
a piece of our sacred journey

don't hide from the truth
don't discount your story
embrace all of the glory
found in the darkness and light
and if the day becomes too blinding
or if in the darkness
you lose sight
of what really matters
and who you really are
there will be helpers and guides
to re-ignite your fire

so don't be afraid
you were made for this life
don't try to control
the ebb and flow of the tide
just ride the wave
use discernment and tact
keep an eye out for evil
don't fall into the traps
you are ready to live now
follow your destiny
explore the depths and the heights
keep your pure spirit free

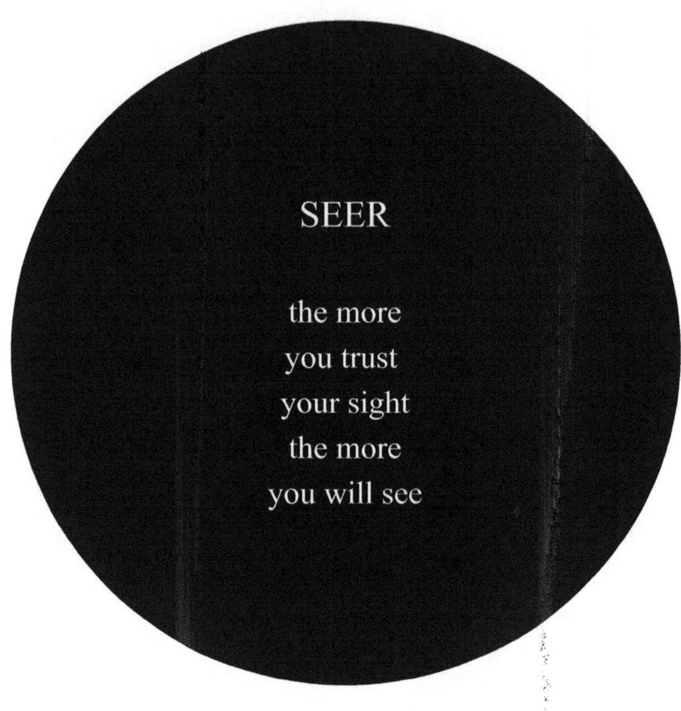

SEER

the more
you trust
your sight
the more
you will see

TOO BOLD FOR ANYONE'S GOOD

i am icarus

i will fly
too close to the sun
every time
with my wax wings
every single time

and each time
i will get closer
and each time as i fall
you will think

wow
that is the most
beautiful shooting star
i've ever seen

THE GIRL CHOOSES HERSELF IN THIS ONE

i still say i love you
like an apology

you say i love you
like the whole world
exists in your heart
and you're giving it all to me

i didn't know
how to be
anything
other than
scared
hesitant
apologetic

you showed me
how to be
brave
sure
powerful

i let my heart break open
a hundred times with you
and found endlessness possibilities
of mosaics we could create

i still don't know
if i deserved you

i still don't know
if i'll ever find
a love like ours

i still imagine
a lake house
with a green house
and your heart
is still my home

it's still too much
to imagine
living life
without you

but i've been
growing these wings
my whole life

day dreaming out windows
living in cages
imagining freedom
in a life that's fully my own

and now I must know
what it's like to
fly

IF NOT YOU THEN WHO

make the art
you want to see
in the world

make the music
you want to hear
in the world

live the love
you want to feel
in the world

with every breath
every word
every sound
every action

live your heart's song

LET GO

beloved
you cannot fly
with the weight of the world
on your shoulders

release your burdens

carrying all that pain
does not serve the world

feel it in your heart
and transmute it

this is your sacred work

wrap your roots
around the core of the earth

reach your branches
to sway in the winds of the heavens

connect deeply to all of life
and have no fear

you are held
supported and loved
beyond what you can possibly imagine

trust the way
and journey on

SOMEWHERE IN THE MIDDLE

there was a time when
i pretended to be a saint

there was a time when
i pretended to be a sinner

but all i ever really wanted to be
was the real true me

CHANGING TIMES

in the
age of information
attention
is the
new currency

CHANCES OF LOVE

there's a longing behind my eyes
that you recognize
that's why it came as no surprise
when you entered my life

we'll always know where to find each other
a dimension deep within our hearts
we have the same hiding place
we have the same backyard
we have the same vision
of a future that could be ours

star crossed lovers
no really it's written in the stars
the night we met comets flew
when the depths of my heart found yours

if words can be more than poetry
if life can be more than hard
if we can open up wider
even when things are falling apart
then maybe true love can be ours

and maybe it's not one thing
one person
one space
one time

maybe the love we dream of
transcends this waking life

SISTERHOOD
behind every
great woman
are more
great women

A NEW MYTHOLOGY

i don't slay dragons
i ride them

my demons only ever
wanted to dance with me
got sad
when i ignored them
got mad
when i caged them
turned ferocious
when i beat them
looked to other people
for the attention
i refused to give them

reclaim them
now they fight for me

newsflash
in 2020 the princess saves herself
the prince plays music and meditates
while she finds her own inner strength

rise up from the ashes sisters
it's time to rebuild the queendom

white witches
they tried to burn us
but we are the phoenix
and we will always rise

this is the story of how i rescued myself
learned how to be me
i am my hand maiden
i am my anointed knight
i am the king of my castle
this is my empire i'm building

my life
my journey
full responsibility

leave your judgments at the door
put your advice on this libra scale
pure intentions are as light as a feather
we'll take them
but there's no room for second hand fear here

i'd tell you to keep it
but you shouldn't either
shake it off together
rise up alongside one another
embody our unique purpose
as manifestations of the same source

focus on your journey
find your own way
your path
your destiny
give me space to work on mine

don't help me unless i ask for it
let me learn how to ask for it

FATE TURNS TO DESTINY

when fate
invites you
to dance
say yes

tell your fears
to sit down
your limiting beliefs
to get out

let the haters'
and the nay sayers'
voices fade away

when fate invites
you to dance
be discerning

your next move
determines your destiny

it's ok
to stumble
on the path
to your
destiny

JUST KEEP GOING

FREE LOVE

every day
i invent a new way
to say
i love you

there are rainbows
in the clouds
that only you and i can see
we watch them dance
and whisper
as you sing
nature perceives
a connection this pure
in a way that man
with his words
finds hard to believe

so my soul negotiates
with my brain
to carve out
more pieces of my heart
to give to you
and i wonder if i had to choose
between freedom and love
which would it be

the butterflies and flowers
laugh at me
isn't it obvious
you can have both

so i ask new questions
and i find new answers
and when i think
i can't possibly love you more
i love you more

and now if there's one thing i know it's that
if i invented a new language
if i stole the stars from the sky
if i walked all over the earth
and kissed every stranger with my eyes
i still wouldn't have the words to describe
the love between you and i

so i leave it all up to fate
i let the pieces fall where they may
i try not to reach out to you
just for a day
but i can't stop day dreaming
about being in your embrace
again i return to surrender
release the old games i used to play
allow the love in my heart to lead the way
and let the words just fall away
no more need to explain
no more hide and seek

just you and me
running wild together
and living the story of
a love that sets us free

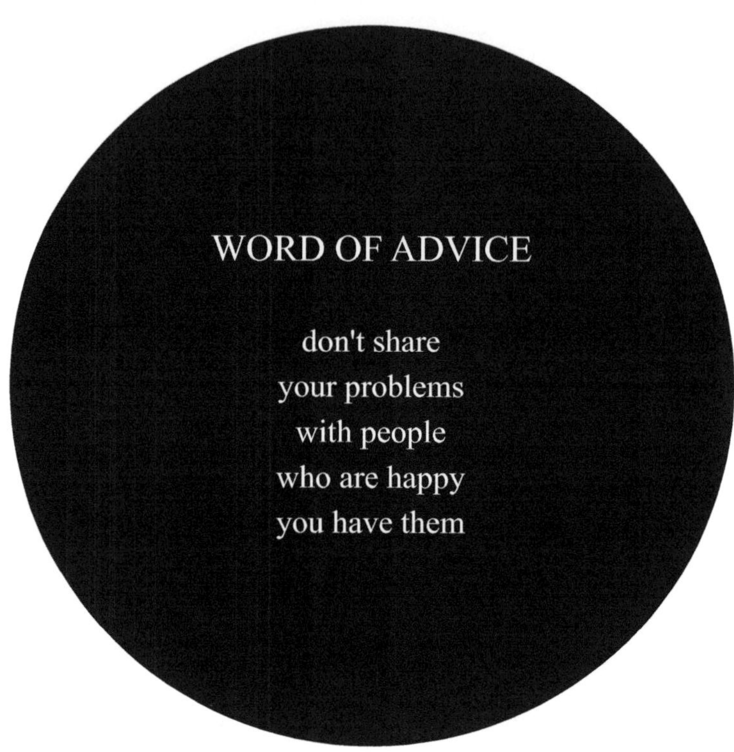
WORD OF ADVICE
don't share
your problems
with people
who are happy
you have them

REASSESS THE MUST DOS

i'm exhausted
from the shoulds
and the ought tos

worn out from
the musts
and the have tos

i'm dropping it all
and just listening to
my own soul's truth

everything just got easier

QUEENDOM

you taught me
how to speak
without words

though your silence
never felt like a reward
more like a punishment

in the end
i'd realize it was neither
just another reality
we got to dance within

and under your weapons
i became a warrior
under fire
i became the phoenix

our relationship was a battlefield
and i was crucified many times
sacrificed in the name of love
until everything that was impure
within me died

and only my truth remained
only my love remained
and when there were no more games
left to be played
our dance was over

and that's when
i found someone
who showed me
that i am more
than just a game
that a relationship
doesn't have to be a war

i found a true king
that showed me

i am a queen

put the weapons away
stop running so fast
stop fighting so hard
and just do
what you were born to do

rule the kingdom

V. nothing can stop a person on a mission

I AM A LIVING PRAYER

i want to touch
the deepest depths

i want to reach
the highest heights

i want to come home
to that perfect center
within me
look in the mirror
and know who i truly am

all illusions fall away
all desires fall away
and here
i am

BYE BYE VEIL

i rip holes in the veil with my teeth
on the seventh day when god rested
the goddess woke up
there's work to be done

thank you for this life
it is beautiful and we broke it
but it doesn't have to stay broken
let's fix it

if we all put our hands together
we could make a web
cover the world with our love
re-invent the garden of eden

do you remember life before the fall
before separation and annexation
before destruction and despair
in between moments
i can still feel it's there

so maybe we could show each other
the truth and love in our hearts
and then maybe we could remember who we really are
and then maybe we could rise up together
mirror the oneness of our souls back to each other

no more separation
no more illusion
no more veil

SOUL MATES

somebody pinch me
i must be dreaming
heart soaring
i must be sleeping
you have me flying
what's the meaning
lost in the clouds
i love this feeling
never want to come down
i can't believe it
you found me
gave me a reason
to have hope
start believing
that true love
never ceases
you kept your promise
i'll keep believing
i'll keep fighting
praying
dreaming
that you and i
will beat the demons
take the throne
and free the people

I'M SORRY / YOU'RE WELCOME

i'm a minute late
11:12
i told myself
i'd stop apologizing
but i like to say
i'm sorry
like a prayer
or sweet embrace
between friends
that are sometimes
lovers
what if they're the same
we're the same
deep inside
where it really matters
what if
instead of saying
i'm sorry
i said
you're welcome
because it's all on purpose
and i don't feel regretful
what I really feel is
grateful

THE VIRUS

fear has a heartbeat
just like love
hope has a heartbeat
just like ignorance

they pulse through the world
like our ancestor's drum
beat beat beat

humans juggle complex feelings
like we're brave enough beings
to handle them
we are

i've seen beautiful miracles performed
in the most horrible situations
hearts rising up together
on wings of love
and yet people do
horrible things here too

so i wonder
would we be given a situation
if we were not strong enough to handle it
if we were
would it make us stronger
or destroy us completely

i dance
in the in-between

in the unknown
i hope
i dream

in darkness
i shine

in chaos
i create

all life is
is opportunity
to grow
to shrink
to choose

will you make the world
a more peaceful place
or will you participate
in her destruction

i see every single person i know
do both
in their own unique way
and so here we co-create
both heaven and hell

but when i look deep
deep into any other humans' eyes
i know

we're all rooting for heaven

WHO AM I? WHO ARE YOU?

i am an instrument for the most high
a tool of the divine
i am a living breathing miracle
the brightest light runs through my spine

i am a walking talking angel
an embodiment of truth and love
reincarnated deities within me
my sights focused on what's above

i am here to spread the light
remind the darkness
it's also divine

i am here to fix what's broken
even surrounded by evil
i shine

A WILDFLOWER IS NOT A WEED

(let her grow)

i picked
the most beautiful flower
hoping
that she would be mine

it felt
so good to hold her
for a moment
i prayed the rest of time

but in my hands
she wilted
no longer who
she was before

i returned her
back to the earth
so she could
come to life once more

GRAND RISING

we speak in energy
you know
good vibes

isn't it all magic
when all we are is
well timed chemical reactions
animated god sparks
in tiny little flesh suits
dancing in the light of life

are you living inspired
does your life enliven you
if not why are you doing it
drop the old stories
channel the pure energy
from your own soul
only then can you truly see another

show up in your full power
so we can each and all mirror
our own version of the same truth
back to one another

uncover
remember
there's a wisdom within
root in it
resurrect it
with your emotions actions and imagination

don't sit in the passenger seat
of your life passive
life passing you by no

you are a creator
living the dance of the highest creatrix
you know the one they call
god
great spirit
the oneness from which we all came
and will eventually all return

this is my spirituality
this is my art
what's yours
own it
as in make it your own
you must own every move
or else you're living a separate fantasy
don't live in fantasy
but oh it's great to visit there

imagination is the vacation
this world is our home
this is where we're rooted
this is what is real
remember the realness together
combining like a perfectly balanced
chemical reaction
because you are
we are
remember

CATCH AND RELEASE

how many futures
have i invested in
that never did come true

forgotten memories
of daydreams
with this breath i honor you

lost lovers
forgotten promises
alternate realities
forsaken friendships
dissolved agreements
and too many abandoned dreams

WILD
sometimes
your friends
are crazy
and you
love them
more
because of it

AGE OF THE GODDESS

free spirited sisters
taking back the earth

i've been here
i recognize
these keepers of the hearth

tend the fires
sow the seeds
share the knowledge
pluck the weeds

lend a hand
take a stand
familiar with rebirth

the old ways cleansed
the wounds are mended
raising the new earth

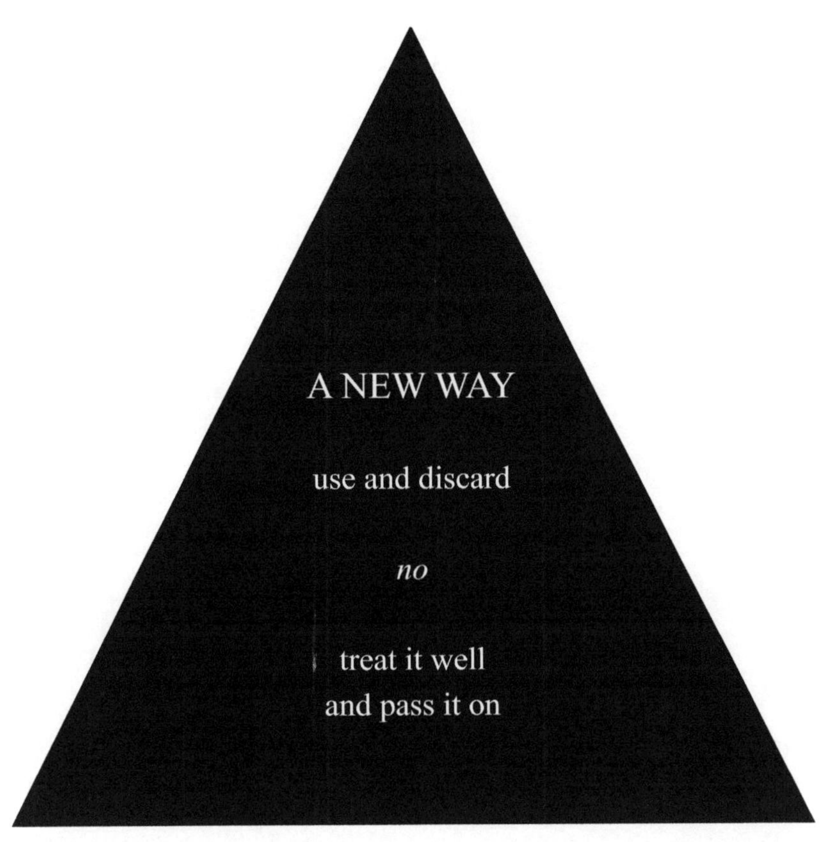
A NEW WAY
use and discard
no
treat it well
and pass it on

THE SKY HASN'T ALWAYS BEEN GRAY

nobody taught them
butterflies can't be kept in cages
but the entire world's a cage
and a butterfly must be kept somewhere
better with this flower than the next

what even is freedom
a fancy ideal
they build nations on
to eventually enslave people

every flower withers
when its season is over
i can't help but think
will it ever bloom again

love is a freedom song
but it's not freedom
just a song

hope floats by
on a blue sky's dream
like the butterfly
that think she's free
while trapped in a paradise like prison
sometimes it's heaven
and sometimes it's hell

you only see a butterfly for a moment
and then she's gone

WAVES OF EMOTION

why do you
prolong your suffering

feelings rise and flow
like waves in the ocean

feel them and let them go
feel them and let them go

you are not
your emotions

you are something
more vast
more brilliant
more profound

you are here
to experience your emotions
but not to identify with them

feel them and let them flow

LOST AND FOUND

i've lost my home
broken compass

i don't know which way to go
so they say
any road will take me there

hitch hiking a ride
on someone else's coat tails
where are you going
anywhere

i can make a home
out of anything

wanderers
are never lost

WHY NOT?

be at peace child
don't wait any longer
for some unknown tomorrow
be at peace now

RECLAIM ME

no matter what
i will reclaim me
destroy all barriers
and false attempts to restrain me
there's no man made law
that can detain me

my soul
is eternal
i burn
what isn't holy
i reject
what's made to hold me
down and back
i break
your so called normal
i refuse
your attempts to control me
i will not go silently
into your dystopian future
i will resist
and i am not alone
in seeing you
and knowing about this

i am a walking revolution
free spirit
there's nothing in existence
that can prevent this

no matter what
i will reclaim me
reclaim the earth
for the creator
break free
from this matrix
and when the evil
goes back to where it came from

we the people will
return heaven to earth

MY MANTRA

next time
i forget
help me
to remember
quickly

MY BODY

my body is not beautiful like the magazines
my body is beautiful like the jungle
no airbrush
no photoshop
no edits
raw and wild
i earned every scar

my body is not beautiful like five days a week at the gym
my body is beautiful like 10 mile hikes through the savannah
like sweat drops
sweet surrender
we made it
take off all your clothes
and jump in the waterfall

my body is not beautiful like the keto diet
my body is beautiful like grab the fruit right off the tree and eat it
like what do you want
follow your heart
like what are you craving
right now

my body is not beautiful like what society wants to see
my body is beautiful like me

DAUGHTER OF THE SEA

daughter of the sea
why do your words
always turn into poems

your emotions so big
your body too little
to hold them

let each salty tear
return you to you

daughter of the sea
you are vast
unreachable
unknown
and yet so familiar

you pull at my heart
as we lead each other
in the dance
of the moon and the tides

daughter of the sea
you are just a drop
in the larger sea
but what a drop you are

powerful and sensual
who can control you
who would want to

daughter of the sea

or are you
a mother
a lover
a teacher
a friend

above definition
outside of time and space

you are the
eternal aphrodite
rising again from
the ocean waves

daughter of the sea
aren't they all your stories

you the queen
of memories
you the goddess
of a thousand names

you the divine feminine heart
and me
you are me

daughter of the sea
daughter of the sea

MY DREAM LIFE WITH YOU

i dreamt that my life was a dream
what other reason could there be
for yellow roses
and daffodils in the yard
and seasons like fall and spring

how else can you explain

the birds that fly to our yard
to watch the sun set
from our favorite tree
and this perfect love
that's blossomed
between you and me
it's all a poem
a song
a dream
reflections
and shadows on the wall
of the deeper love
that's flourishing
between you and me

for all of life is an act
and we act out the deeper themes
of a dream we dreamt in another dream
when we knew for certain
undoubtedly
that this life and everything in it
is more perfect than it may seem

but to forget
is to take up the journey
the courage
the bravery
to face uncertainty
and find new answers
to the same old questions
of who we are
and what we can be

so we search and we find
in circles
as life unfolds
the greater mysteries
and i thank you and the one we pray to
for infinitely blessing me

for my heart found a resting place
sweet solace
a break from the tragedies
a home
in this love that's grown
through lifetimes
between all the versions
of you and me

alas i've found my favorite dream
to sit with you
under this great oak tree
to feel the cool breeze
and hear the sweet songs
from some other lovers' dreams

THAT GIRL

and so
that girl
became a woman
and that woman
became a queen
and that queen
became a goddess
and that goddess realized
deep down inside
she would always be
that girl

DUALITY

a hater
can find anything
to hate
about any situation

a lover
can find anything
to love
about any situation

and this is how
we decide
if life is hell
or if it is heaven

DO YOU SEE WHAT I SEE?

the wind tells a story
can you hear it

all your life
you've searched
for something
that's inside you

doubted god
then heard her
in your heartbeat
saw him
in the clouds
felt it
on the wind
became one
with the earth

all of creation
is singing

can you hear it

the song you wrote
before you came here

can you feel it

all of life
is moving with you

dancing birds

it wouldn't be the same
without you

god's breath
is in your breath
life's heartbeat
is in your heartbeat
the goddess' dance
is in your dance

every moment is new

we painted a story
for you

can you see it
can you see it

ABUNDANCE MANTRA

i am abundant
even when the world is not
i am abundant
even when everything around me is not
i am abundant
in a million undefinable ways

abundance flows to me
and through me
and out from me
to wherever it is most needed

i am abundant
like mother earth is abundant
i am abundant
life father sky is abundant
i am abundant
and i create abundance everywhere i go

PEACE MANTRA

i am peaceful
even when the world is not
i am peaceful
even when everything around me is not
i am peaceful
in a million undefinable ways

peace flows to me
and through me
and out from me
to wherever it is most needed

i am peaceful
like mother earth is peaceful
i am peaceful
life father sky is peaceful
i am peaceful
and i create peace everywhere i go

I AM MY ANCESTOR'S REDEMPTION

why does the word white
taste like poison
feel like an insult
hurt like something broken

how can i feel proud
of a lineage of conquest
rape murder and destruction
or its more socially acceptable descendants
of segregation suppression discrimination
crude jokes and superiority complexes
no longer so socially acceptable

white supremacy
we see you now with both eyes open
white supremacy
your time is up

all the rainbow warriors
the children of all colors of the earth
rise up now and reclaim her

white supremacy
you did your best
and we're still standing
now let us show you equality
what love peace and symbiosis with the earth
is all about

i am white
so i rip this guilt from my chest
it does nothing to save my cherokee ancestors
honor the tears that well up in my eyes
when i remember finding
my four times great grandmother's place of death
trail of tears kansas

hand in hand with
the descendants of those who were stolen from their land
and the descendants of those who had their land stolen
and the descendants of those who stole the land

we the people

we will not apologize
for our ancestor's pain
but maybe we can heal
our ancestor's mistakes
honor our ancestor's sacred stories
the part each person played
in a twisted broken history

we will make it right now
for those who came before us
for those who will come after us
for those who are here now
for the earth
we will make it right

AFTER THE STORM PASSES

how does your heart find healing
your body find rest
your mind find peace
when all you've known is battle

there are people whose lives are still wars
their waking reality is a nightmare
they have never known peace
so how can you call yourself free

when you live in a nation
built off of slavery and segregation
where your fellow citizens are still in chains
poverty homelessness discrimination
how can you call yourself free

when your neighbor is trapped by the system
when they've become numb to their pain
can't even dream anymore about an escape
when they've accepted some twisted fate
how can you call yourself free

are you really free
when invisible cages exist in all of our minds
with a thousand invisible keys
are we really free

A WORSHIP SONG

life has highs
and it has lows
but through it all
your love remains

i drown in sorrow
i wallow in pain
but through it all
your love remains

i rise in joy
i celebrate
and through it all
your love remains

through every change
through every change
i give thanks
your love remains

RISE ROOTED

roots in the earth
it's safe for you to be here
unfolding the magic of the seed
discovering what you hold dear

the magic deep within you
blooming towards the light
the wisdom of your spirit
growing wings and taking flight

your mind knows so much
and it's a blessing to discover
your body knows deep secrets
she's waiting for you to uncover

you heard the call from deep within
to find a slower pace
and as you listen closer
your intuition shows its face

it's always been with you
as a subtle nudge or a gentle tap
a longing to hold yourself
a feeling that it's safe to open up

you've helped so many souls
to see their own soul's light
to know the value they provide
to remember their birthright

now you learn to give
that same love and grace to yourself
to value your own inner knowing
and nurture your own inner child

your imagination beckons you closer
remember me my dear friend
your creativity is shining through
it's time to begin again

so you'll rise rooted
feet grounded in the earth
a new adventure awaits you
a new you is waiting to be birthed

another layer of your destiny
shows its glowing face
it's safe for you to be here
you're in the perfect place

FREE AUTHENTIC ME

let everything
that is not
authentically me
melt away
fall away
drop to the ground
back to the earth

let everything that is not mine
return to where it came from

i am free
always have been
always will be

ONE MOUNTAIN

on the road
up the mountain
every vendor
tries to sell you
their special drink
in their special cup

when you reach
the top of the mountain
you see that
all the sages
drink the same drink
and they use their hands
for a cup

BODY TRUST

when my body
says rest
i rest

when my body
says rise
i rise

these are the cycles
of nature

i trust
in the patterns of life

GUPT

portals to other places
memories of other times
i hear ancient stories
when i look into your eyes

forgotten wisdom
who buried the truth
it's time now to remember
the answers inside of you

you are the key
you are the message
the hidden door
look inside discover
what the earth has in store

outside of logic
somewhere beyond time
the whispers of your heart
know more than your mind

it's all a sacred balance
this beautiful dance of life
there's only one now moment
and look now it's the time

VI. in the end there was love

RARE

what does it feel like
to love with your whole heart
to release all expectations
to give and receive freely
to drop all boundaries and barriers
to let yourself fall in love fully
to be in love and live in love
every moment of your life

could you be so brave
to give yourself this gift
to give the world this gift

the truest and rarest life
lived in complete
unconditional
love

ERGO SUM

i think
thoughts
but
i am
not
the thinker
of those
thoughts

the thoughts
are being
thought
through
me

FULL SPECTRUM ACCEPTANCE

there are
hard things
and
there are
great things
in every single day

i will learn to
see them all
and
love life
all the same

A PROMISE

i want to find a million ways
to hold your hand
fly to the moon together
and make a home
wherever we land

i want to look at you
every day
and fall a little more
in love

the earth shows me
more of her face
every day
the universe reveals
more of its secrets to me
every day
god expands in my heart
more and more
every day

and i will come to know you
and love you more
every day

ICE QUEEN

there are worlds unseen within me
in the cold chill of winter
i can hear them beating
the drum inside my heart
is it my ancestors' song

the land is calling me home
return return return
back to the earth
but my blood freezes
as i reach for the sun
trapped by the clouds
and my soul trapped too
inside this body

snow falls silently outside in the quiet of winter
while i live inside four walls i call home
and forget what it feels like
to rest my belly on the earth

we've learned to distract ourselves
with the worlds we've constructed inside black boxes
and fall into stories inside pages made from paper
of the trees that died so we could build new worlds

everyday the world is new
everyday i am new
shapeshifter
something ancient and futuristic
between my two eyes pulling me deeper

remember remember remember
who you have been
remember remember remember
who you will be

infinite energy swirling
i drop every story
surrender into the great mystery
a million worlds are born
a million worlds are destroyed
within me

and all i really know is
i am here now
being
beating
breathing
the question who am i
matters less than the fact that i am

inside and outside
the same themes re-birthing
ice
now fire
now ice
now fire

outside of time i see
the perfect dance of life
and somehow i've become
the perfect vessel to contain it all
a human being

2%

they made my eyes green
so if i ever thought i was
of ocean
or sky
of distant galaxies
or of the night
i would remember
i am of the Earth

FOR THOSE FROM SOMEWHERE BETTER

she was too good
for this world
too kind
too soft
too real

in a world full of quick fixes
and fast cars
cheap food
and fake smiles

she was something true

she was too good
for this world
and so
when she couldn't fight anymore
when she couldn't shine anymore
the world let her rest
and this is how she won

the world allowed her to rest
and she went home
to where the pure ones belong
to where the pure ones are safe
to where the pure ones are free

IT'S HEALED WHEN IT STOPS HURTING

open up that buried book titled
healed
give it a second look
what waits to be
revealed

there's always more to discover
in the depths of yourself
lost parts to recover
in the dungeon of yourself

open up the wounds
pain buried deep within
pick out the little splinters
still left under your skin

clean out the poison
from an unknown incident
when did this pain begin
take root in a once pure heart
can it be pure again

wash clean
like god-forgiven sins
like bleach white innocence
like you know remember when

trace back the traumas
connect the dots with scars
remember lost constellations
eyes once filled with stars

refill the well
with the magic of yourself
everything heals in time
but through time it's healing still

relight the fire
look it started to go dim
but by reclaiming your truth
you start to shine again

maybe it will always hurt
somewhere a little bit
but when you do the inner work
it gets easier to deal with

truly look inside
discover what lies within
gain the strength
to hold the pain
and shine your light
unburdened

SING CHILD SING

this is for the little girl
who says
she hates the sound of her own voice

i hope you grow up
and remember how to roar

you think you're tone deaf
but really
you haven't grown into your big range
a range that captures the distance
between soft and subtle i love yous
and violent destructive i hate yous
and everything in between

little girl
i hope you grow up
and remember how to sing

oh you
you think your voice is too shrill
but you just haven't found your own inner peace
one day they'll tell you that
your voice is soothing for the soul
and maybe you won't believe it
until you've heard it 100 times
but that song of peace is inside you
even now

little girl
i hope you grow up
and remember how to be at home in your body
you will i know
because you have i know

but for now you laugh and you laugh
and they say they can hear your laugh for miles
too loud
tone it down
but you hold the joy of the universe in your breath
and how can that ever be tamed

little girl
i hope you grow up
and remember there's no reason to ever dim your shine

you are powerful
you are right
you are true

little girl
i hope you grow up
and remember how to be you

A PAUSE FOR A PRAYER

dear god

thank you for being here for me
even when i didn't think you were
even when i didn't know you were
even when i wasn't here for myself

thank you for always
looking out for me
and watching over me

thank you for being inside me
being next to me
and being all around me all the time

please help me to see you more
in everything

i love you
and i want to do more of your work
in the world

please show me
how i can best be of service

increasing harmony
peace truth love

amen

THE POSSIBILITIES OF YOU

what if
i told you that

you have the power
of a supernova inside you

god breathes through your body
and lives through your life

you are pure love
manifesting in human form

every moment is a miracle
hidden in plain sight

what if

you could wake up
to the wonder of life
and the power inside you

what then

SACRED WARRIOR

sacred warrior
when did you
put down your bow
broke your arrows
buried your sword
dropped your shield

when did you
stop praying
at the altar of your soul
believed somebody else's lies
that your way of praying wasn't right

when did you
forget your mission
grew tired of fighting
retired
ignored the soul hunger
soul calling
come back to us
save us
protect us
you're our only hope of a meaningful life

why did you abandon
the only purpose you've ever known
were the dangers of the road too terrible
when tempted with the comforts of home

sacred warrior
why did you stop fighting
deciding
that the war between good and evil
wasn't worth your time
maybe it was all just
a fabrication of your mind

sacred warrior
why did you stop believing
stop giving of yourself
stop grieving
stop seeking a better world
stop bleeding
abandoning the purpose
that kept your heart beating

can't you see that
fighting for what you believe in
gives you a reason
to keep on breathing
that peace is in the process
of just simply being
not fighting your destiny
but gracefully surrendering
to who you came here to be

a sacred warrior

MAIDEN TO MOTHER

i take my abandoned dreams
down to the river
lifeless forgotten things
that just wanted wings
to fly

i cradle them
like they were miscarriages
aborted fetuses
i'm so sorry
i couldn't bring you to life

the choices
the pain
the responsibility
of a mother
no words can describe

but as i sit here at the river
i see all my sisters
burying their dead dreams
laying their pain to rest
each in their own way
and i know i am not alone

i just pray one day
i bring something to life in the world
and feel worthy of the name
mother

UNDERWORLD

deep in the dungeon
i set myself free
all those tortured
aspects of me
that just wanted to be
part of the whole
living in harmony

GUIDED BY FORCES GREATER

you found
what you were
looking for
of course
you always do
because you live
in the flow of life
and so life
looks out
for you

REVOLUTIONS

movements
are made
out of thousands of
small actions

people
who want to see
a change

voices
crying out
as if part of
a larger voice

justice
we demand
justice

liberty
to see the earth
and all of its people be
as they were created to be
free

IN MEDITATION

meet me at the tree
in the center of your soul

take a deep breath
in the breaking dawn
with the glow of the sun
so we can really feel
the end of the night
stars fading
birds chirping
eyes opening

a celebration
of the true source of life

but do not lose yourself
in the worship
of reflections
tricks of the mind
and pulling of the heart
away from the truth
that beats steadily in
your own blood
your own skin
your own bones

the ego wants the throne
to be the one
the only one

or else
to be left alone
as none
part of nothing

to make a god
out of the sun
or a goddess
out of the moon

but there is a spark of light
in everything
and this same light
is in me too

so i drop the old games
the stories
the make believe
the searching and striving
for something greater
realizing that
i am no less and no more
than the sun or the moon
the wind or the ocean
the stars or the trees
the plants or the animals
the gods or any other being

for i too
have the source of life
inside of me

YOU GET YOU

you can't solve the riddle
of other people's lives
the only shot you've got
is solving the riddle
of your own

WE HEAL TOGETHER

don't forget that
colonizers
first had to be
colonized

decolonize everything

CALL TO ACTION

for so long
the pain paralyzes you
what to do

what to do
about a broken world
afraid to make a move
to create more pain
more violence
more heartbreak
to be wrong
and do wrong

for so long
you did nothing
because you had no idea
what to do

the quiet fire
in your belly burning
i want to stop the hurt
i want to make it better
i want to erase the pain
as if it were as easy
as pressing
undo
backspace
delete

but there's
no magic bullet
no healing word
no easy button

so what to do
when the pain eats away at you
when the pain of the world weighs
and weighs on you
and you don't know what to do

i can no longer sit with it
feel it and do nothing

before the weight crushes you
before the pain buries you
headline after headline
more devastating news
before the devastation
overcomes you
find something
anything
you
can do

A PURPOSE FOR LIFE

what could be
more important
than this

the love
we give
freely
to each other
from our hearts

TIME AGAIN

my heart
wants to know
my soul
wants to know
if it's time
to surrender
the false illusion
of control

DIVINE CHILD

the magic has always
been inside you

when did you forget
you were born with
everything you need
to love yourself

you are not of a broken world
but of a divine world
and you will learn to love
everything that's broken within you
so that it becomes divine too

now i can give myself the love i wasn't able to
when i thought i was too awkward to love
when i thought i was too much to love
when i thought i was unworthy of love

now i can give myself the love
i looked for in other people
no longer needing external validating
crowds cheering
people gathering
ego gratifying
complimenting
from other people
also looking for love outside of themselves

the soul hunger for acceptance
can only be found through accepting thyself

and knowing this with the mind
is very different
than feeling it in the heart
the body
the soul
going back in time
and giving that little girl
the love and acceptance
she couldn't give to herself

now i can rest
in this quiet center within me
in this peaceful center
filled with love
in this loving center
where i can trust
in this safe center
where i am home
in this perfect center
within my soul

divine child
the divine mother
and divine father
love you in a way
nobody else can
nobody else
but yourself

TELL ME ABOUT YOU

i want to know if you can hold
the fact that you've come so far
and that you still have so much further to go
in the same breath

i want to know if you're prepared
to look your failures in the face
and know that you're just as worthy of losing it all
as you are of gaining it all

i want to know if you're able
to dance with the full spectrum of life
and say nothing but thank you
thank you and thank you again

i want to know if you're ready
to lay down your ego
and invite your soul to lead
refusing to believe
all the other voices that tell you
your soul's truth isn't right

i want to know if you plan
to do more than just exist
i want to know if you plan
to truly
freely and fiercely
live

ALIGNMENT MANTRA

i attract
all things to me
meant for me

i release
all things from me
not meant for me

CHANGING TIDES PT. 2 (SOUL MATES)

meet me at high tide
on the cliff side

speak to me about
eternity
and destiny
and what it means
to find your perfect match
to search your whole life
for that one being
to believe beyond all reasonable doubt
that they're out there
to stare at the sea
and search through the stars
to watch the clouds change form
and the years pass by
to see your chances dwindle
with each glance from a new stranger's eyes

say the words
soul mates
twin flames
partners till the end of time
a match made in heaven
arranged by the universe
fulfilling god's grand design

a lifetime of longing is over

no need to search the sand
for that one special shell
no need to search the sky
for my special star

i found the place
that i belong
home
in the curve of your arms

remind me how lucky
no
how blessed
we are
to find each other
here
again
in this now
fleeting moment

most things
are constantly changing

but some things
forever
stay the same

CALL TO REAL ACTION

how long
will you stay silent
until the words
spill out of your mouth

how can you bare
to see your brother suffer
and your sister lost to herself

don't you think it's time
we do something

stand up
i mean take a real stand

don't you think it's time
we freed ourselves
from the disease
that's captured our land

STAY TRUE
people will not like
the fact that
you're so powerful
be so powerful anyways

MOMMA WISDOM

my mom kept me wild
praise the lord

taught me that
it's ok to speak my truth
in fact it's safe to do so
it's ok to be bold and powerful
to have my own way of doing things
to want to change the world

someone told her that
she'd have to break my spirit
like a horse
if i was going to have any chance
of fitting into this world
but my mom she left me wild
taught me how to smile
taught me how to be kind
to respect my elders
and how to love
like really truly love
but she left my spirit wild

my mom told me
people won't always be able to hold you
they won't always like you
you'll walk into a room
and someone will hate you
cause your eyes are green
or cause you're tall

or cause
they'll have their reasons
but that's not your problem
love yourself anyway
and if you can love them anyway
then you have unlocked a secret to life

she told me
my sisters are my friends for life
that nothing and nobody
will ever be able to destroy our bond
that friends come and go
but sisters are forever

my mom told me
by giving love away freely
you become a spiritual millionaire

she was right
about it all

my mom taught me everything
that i love about myself
and i learned how to love the rest

for this i rejoice forever
in family
i have been truly blessed

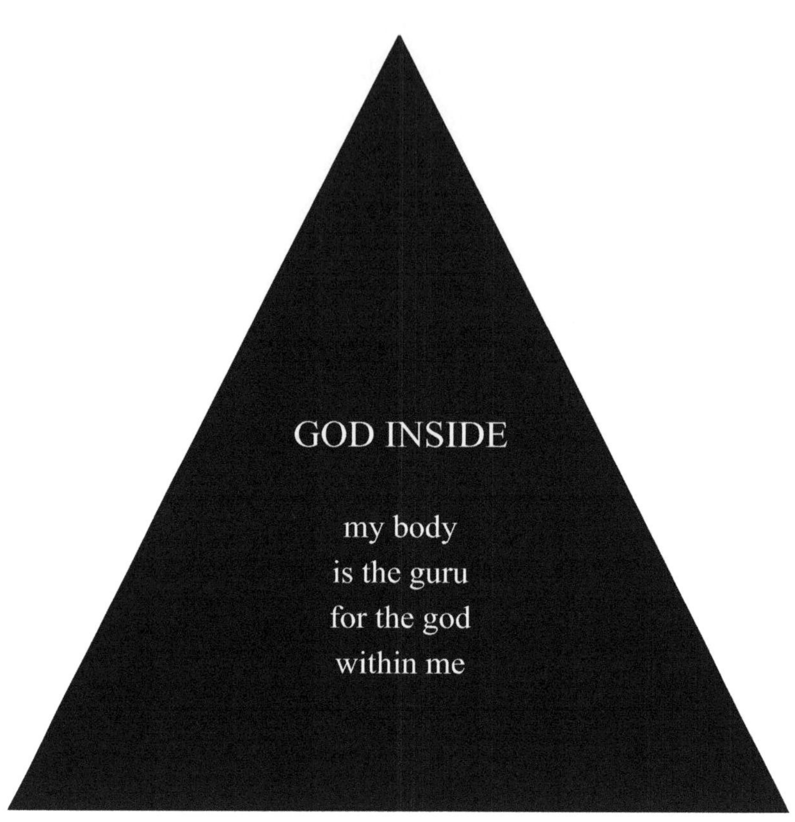

GOD INSIDE
my body
is the guru
for the god
within me

STEP BY STEP

i don't want to be somebody
who has it all
figured out

i want to be somebody
who is figuring it out
every day

THE POWER OF FLUIDITY

i'm shapeshifting
jumping timelines
i'm not the same person
you spoke to last week

the phoenix
knows nothing else
but to be reborn

life
death
rebirth
and repeat
and repeat

how many lives
have i lived
in this one life

my purpose
pulsing in my heart
and shifting too

go here
now here
do this
now that

i listen
ear to the ground
of the earth

how much more silent
can i get
to hear my own voice

how much more present
can i get
to receive my own soul

show me
guide me
where do we go next

END TIMES

an eye for an eye
no wonder
the world is blind

living in hatred
so far
from god's grand design

bombed nations
bomb nations
and free states
deport refugees

utopia reduced
to dirt dust and ashes
look around
we're so far from free

when one country's
holocaust
turns into another country's
occupation
when wars are fought
in the name of god
while we sit and wait
for a more peaceful revelation

that $10 shirt
keeps developing countries
in poverty
but people can barely afford
their own rent
paycheck to paycheck
is also suffering

we walk right by
the homeless guy
thinking what did he do
to get in this mess
but did he fail society
or is he another symptom
of society's distress

there's no simple solutions
when passing a bill through congress
is so convoluted

but the world
is crying and bleeding
and her children
are desperately seeking

where is the cure for the apocalypse

ETERNAL SPRING INSIDE

it's always spring
in that corner
of your heart
when the rain
floods the river
and the tree
loses its leaves
when the sky
erupts in violent thunder
when it's no longer safe
to sit outside

there's a quiet corner
a silent center
a safe space
in your heart
where it is always
spring

CONTEMPLATION OF MOOL MANTRA

Originally written in Gurmukhi by Guru Nanak Ji
Contemplative understanding by Courtney Force
Waheguru Ji Ka Khalsa Waheguru Ji Ke Fateh

there is a oneness
that we all come from

it is the eternal truth
that created us all

it does not contain
any fear
or any hate

this energy is eternal
and self-sustaining
outside of time
beyond birth and death

connect with it
through the grace
of the guru inside you

meditate on this
again and again

UPLEVEL

timelines converging

the next highest version of me
is ready to step through

welcome home the queen

the one from my visions
the one from my dreams
the one whose holy purpose
is to set my spirit free

quantum leaps

those that don't believe
have never tasted magic
have never heard their own hearts sing
have never received a whisper on the wind
or an answer from the trees

but when
you surrender
old stale beliefs
you make room
for a new reality
the fresh identity
of who you're
meant to be

upgraded dna

armageddon
and
ascension
happen
at the same
time

your frequency
decides
which you perceive

and i want you
to join me
on the higher path
of ancient prophecy

can you let go
of the pain
and stagnation
of a lower frequency

step into
a new vibration
and claim your destiny

LOST AND FOUND

if you don't find
what you seek
inside of you

you won't find it
anywhere else

STAY HERE NOW

the present moment
is the only place
where the magic is

CHOICES TO BE MADE

all the time
the stars are dancing
shifting tectonic plates
nothing is stagnant
even the trees are breathing
can you hear them

you and i
are dancing an age old dance
cells dividing and dying
become part of the oneness again

i am the phoenix rising
you are the dragon flying
the pure remain unburnt in the fire
gold remains gold

the soul is not afraid
of what kills the ego
the eternal soul
has not a single thing to fear

we are stars
shining
exploding
vibrating

we are the rare few
who tasted eternity
and lived to tell the story
translate the great mystery
and welcome our siblings home

this is sacred work
don't you know
no elevator pitch
no tag line
no 5 year plan
can encompass this magic
that we are birthing
in those subtle silent moments
when our eyes lock
and we know
we have always been home

the whole world is transforming
timelines shifting
are you ready
for the next golden age
or shall we keep sleeping
peaceful resting waiting
a few more centuries
in darkness

MY SOUL MATE TOLD ME

you don't move
the way they do

you move
with spirit

soul dancer

IN CONCLUSION

the soul's dance
is never done

we are made
of something
eternal

when all things
fade away
it is love
that remains

and we are
living breathing
dreaming feeling
doing knowing
thinking believing
and being just being
love

don't you think
it's time
you started acting
like what you really are
love

it's all just love
and you are love
remember

VII. there will always be love

remember?

www.ingramcontent.com/pod-product-compliance
Ingram Content Group UK Ltd.
Pitfield, Milton Keynes, MK11 3LW, UK
UKHW041636190726
13854UKWH00006B/2532

9 798218 027605